EVERYBODY DESERVES FINANCIAL SECURITY

Theriault Editions

I0493438

Author: Marc Thériault

Copyright 2016

ISBN-13:
978-1534774117

ISBN-10:
1534774114

Link to the author: (Marc Thériault) on amazon.com

Legal submission Quebec national library 2016
Legal submission Canadian national library 2016

I dedicate this book to the divine and creative spirit that each of us has within us.

Table of Contents

Introduction

I have been passionate about finance for the past 25 years and as a representative in this domain my objective has always been to assist people to the best of my ability to make their daily lives easier with regard to their finances.

During my career, I have traveled hundreds of thousands of kilometers to serve my customers and I am grateful to have had this privilege, along with some wonderful experiences which have made their mark on my own personal development.

My aim is to promote prosperity for everyone who has the desire to change their life and destiny, and, as a result, to help the world with these accumulated riches, thanks to the principles set out in this book.

In 2013, I attended a conference in New York, during which it was mentioned that our finances are 80 % linked to our psychology and only 20 % to more mechanical functions. I was amazed by this discovery since in my mind everything was based on logic and left little space for creativity or the power of the mind.

I am now aware, however, that the problem lies mainly in our consciousness and essentially with resources that we often believe to be limited.

It is for this reason that my book partly addresses the system of beliefs, for it is true that we need to modify our thought structure with regard to this energy that we call money.

I wish you great happiness and affluence in your lives so that you can change your vision of yourself and your fellow human beings with the objective of being ever more passionate about your personal finances.

CHAPTER 1

Creating Your Riches

Be Aware of Your Prosperity

To be aware of prosperity is fundamental and universal and, without knowing it, we have the means of making our riches even more fruitful.

The heavens are full of magnificent stars and Nature overflows with colors and trees which yield their fruit in abundance.

Each and every one of us has a part to play in this adventure of earthly prosperity. We must make the riches that we already possess become even more productive. For example, when a businessman comes up with a great idea to start a company, not only does he use his own talents but he also seeks to employ other talented people who can assist him in his venture. Afterwards, he buys the necessary equipment to put together his project. In the long term this experience leads to the creation of riches both for himself and for others.

We have infinite possibilities. We just need to identify exactly how we want to manage our individual wealth and also global wealth if the opportunity arises.

Why Poverty?

Why is it that poverty continues to exist in our society?

I was born in a capitalist country where certain people have been able to develop their talents by taking advantage of free enterprise, though sometimes with the feeling that they have done so at the expense of others. We have made the distribution of wealth more complicated, thereby creating a difficult situation for everyone.

Governments have not found a solution for putting an end to poverty in all countries, since it has existed throughout the centuries and continue to exist today.

Fortunately, we can still count on the help of certain brilliant and resolute businessmen.

I understand poverty and the injustice it brings. My aim today, as an author, is to try and find the means to create prosperity for the good of all.

As I grow older, I have become aware of the fact that it is no use counting on governments or wealthy institutions to get rich, either individually or collectively.

Do some tests yourself. For instance, try holding out your hand in a shopping mall or on the sidewalk. You will soon realize that dollars do not rain down from the heavens! Perhaps, with a bit of luck, someone will take pity on you and will give you a few coins. If you play the lottery, you might also have a rare stroke of luck and win something, although the majority of people who play games of chance remain poor since they relinquish their personal power of increasing their wealth to the luck of the game.

The creation of prosperity can only happen if you manage what you already possess more efficiently, or if you create new products or services that are useful to society as a whole.

We call this process added value to people's lives.

Look For Four Inner Resources

To gain prosperity it is first of all necessary to consider yourself as someone who is inwardly rich. Prosperity cannot simply be summed up as money. Your individual potential, possibilities and talents can be transformed into affluence for yourself and for others.

It is tempting to let oneself be trapped by the comparison and competition conveyed by modern society, but this can only hinders your real inner resources for the future. Because of this, people believe that they are incapable of getting what they want in life.

Finally, some people take the path of self-destruction, with alcohol, gambling or drugs, simply because nobody ever told them that they had hidden potential. Everybody is creative in some way or another and, if you see yourself as someone who is constructive, this treasure concealed deep inside you must surely emerge someday.

There is a fitting proverb which says, "give a man a fish and you feed him for a day; teach a man to fish and you feed him for a lifetime". A person may go bankrupt but nobody can succeed in taking away his awareness of his own inner resources.

By searching your heart and mind you will come to understand better and better the principle of true prosperity and you will therefore never be poor.

The Story of The Poor Man, The False Rich Man Who is Searching for Himself, and The True Rich Man

Let us now analyze the poor man's distress. The poor man always sees himself as lacking something and he shouts out his frustration to whoever is willing to hear. Because he compares himself to other people and cannot obtain what our consumer society is constantly offering him he feels trapped in a vicious circle and does not know how to get out of it. Even if he has a rise in salary he is still destitute as compared with others and this makes him envious.

Why do the poor remain poor?
Simply because they do not see that prosperity is above all internal and not external.

In short, we should never wait to see what the outside world has to offer us but, on the contrary, ask ourselves how we can contribute towards the happiness around us.

Remember that you are worth more than anything that exists in material society. Trust your inner strength and you will see that your outside world will prosper in all the different spheres of your life.

It is essential to remain aloof from this materialistic society which renders us financially dependent. The poor man can get out of his situation if he searches within himself. He will find a treasure or sometimes simply an idea that could change his destiny. Everything is inside him and, whatever his origins may be, he has the possibility to create a new service or product that can contribute to the well-being of all. Potential for prosperity exists in each and every one of us.

Let us now take the example of the false rich man. Rich on the outside but with an inner poverty that is sometimes quite alarming, the *false rich man'* always wants to possess more than he has because somewhere at the back of his mind he is conscious of the fact that there is something missing, an inner void. He is terrified at the idea of losing his money and he shuts himself away from others. Indeed he suffers from a kind of continual poverty in spite of all his wealth.

The false rich man seeks to satisfy his desires by continually buying property and companies by consuming. The day he discovers that his resources are inside him, he will at last be able to rest at ease without having to continually prove to himself that he is rich and without having to show off his riches to other people. He will then be able to help his fellow human beings to progress in the same way, thereby creating greater prosperity for everyone.

As for the *true* rich man, he has understood the principle of prosperity. He has worked and invested his time and his money. Once he has fully understood the steps leading to his ascent, he can gradually teach all those who are inclined to listen to him.

In sharing his knowledge and his numerous experiences, he rejects the prospect of becoming an old and lonely rich man.

I have read various autobiographies written by rich people. With the help of luck or chance happenings these people have become even richer in all domains, material as well as spiritual. It is as if they have mastered the principle of 'giving and receiving.

The three categories of people mentioned above can be found all over the world. Let it be understood that I am not here to cast judgment, but to help you to prosper. I am simply aware of the economic injustices and social differences that have always existed.

I wish you all prosperity - and if you succeed in acquiring it in this world, so much the better!

Having said that, your inner resources will always be worth more than all the material wealth in the world. When you are really happy in your heart and mind, then you are truly rich.

It is obvious that your financial prosperity will only develop thanks to your own personal actions and not otherwise. The personal nature depends entirely on you. In our capitalist system, nobody can take action in your stead.

Many people find this system hard because we get the impression that only a handful of people actually succeed. The gulf gets wider and wider between rich and poor. Nothing is perfect, but we must make the most of being fortunate enough to live in a world which abounds in possibilities.

Beliefs About Money

The many beliefs concerning anything that involves money can destroy your well-being and your relationship with money.

The following beliefs are dangerous and can in certain cases ruin your happiness and your zest for living:
- Rich people go to hell

- Rich people are bandits

- Money is dirty

- Money can't buy happiness
- Money is dangerous and a sign of corruption

- Money is destroying the planet

- Money creates more and more poverty

Ask yourself the following question: what is my belief concerning the fact that I have always had plenty of money in my life and also the education received from my parents about money? In this way, you will probably be able to remove the mental blocks that for a long time have kept you in a negative mindset and tapped all your energy.

I propose the following exercise:

Write down on a blank page everything you believe with regard to money. This exercise can help you change your destiny and your relationship with money for good.

Make a list of all the beliefs that currently poison your life and replace them with new beliefs and the following assertions:

- I deserve to make my fortune and I like myself

- I deserve prosperity in all its forms

- I was born to be rich

- I master wealth

- I am the creator of prosperity for myself and for others

- I am a person who perseveres and I believe in my financial potential

- I can multiply financial assets

How to Create Affluence

"If we want to have more, we must begin by managing more efficiently what we already have in our hands and our minds."

Nowadays, people are better informed about the mechanism that we call prosperity. Television and other media show us numerous people who have started off in life with virtually nothing and who have built financial empires. Are these people more astute than the average person? I think not. Some of them have no university diploma. What makes them so different is their desire to earn more and to contribute to the world in general.

Warren Buffett, who is one of the most successful investors in the world, has bought businesses cheaply, but these businesses already had the potential to grow and prosper and he has since had the know-how to manage them efficiently.

Such investors could have thrown in the towel right at the start, but their patience has enabled them to win their bet – namely, to reach a turnover of a billion dollars.

They are a remarkable example, but in principle I do not believe that the majority of those wishing to make a fortune succeed so easily. We all have our own strengths but we are not all financial gurus or IT wizards like Bill Gates.

To create wealth you have to believe in yourself and take the plunge!

Financial Independence

Is this such a difficult path to take?

Most of us believe that people who are financially independent have a bank account with around a million dollars in it, but this is generally not the case. Let us suppose that I am a rich father and that I give each of my sons, Andrew, Luke and Billy, who are in their twenties, a weekly sum of 100 $. At the end of the week we get together and I ask them to give me full details of what they did with their money.

First of all I ask Andrew: "What did you do with your 100 $?" "I've got no money left," he replies, "because I bought some sunglasses for 90 $ and two beers at the bar with the other 10 $. And I owe 20 $ to my best friend, so I would need a bit more, Dad..."

I ask Luke the same question and this is his reply: "I bought some tools for 60 $ to fix my car and a book on mechanics for 15 $. Then I spent 10 $ at the cinema and the other 15 $ I put in the bank."

As he has clearly understood the question, Billy immediately replies, "I bought a book on finance for 25 $ and a sweater for another 25 $. I put 25 $ in the bank and the remaining 25 $ in a special account towards buying a house later on. But I would need another 100$, Dad."

In these three situations, we can see that each son has spent his money according to his personality and in his own way. The first one is going to find that times get harder as life goes on because he does not act in a manner that will create prosperity. The second one will do better and the third will get very rich, as we can see from his method of managing his money.

However, at the beginning, all three sons received the same amount of money – 100$. To create wealth, it suffices to manage one's assets efficiently. Indeed, it is by good management that one can become financially independent.

With the same sum of money, it is only the methods and behaviour of each individual that differ. We live in a free society where we are encouraged to consume more than ever before. Everything is beautiful, practical and enticing. All we need is a computer and a credit card and we can buy anything we fancy. It is too easy!

Improving our lifestyle by getting into debt seems a fair enough solution at first, but has to be excluded in the long run. Young couples starting out in life are liable to be tempted into spending money and they consequently find themselves landed with huge debts.

Even older people who have become accustomed to a comfortable way of life and want to continue at the same pace have to constantly try to economize so that they can be prepared for any unexpected eventuality.

The problem at the root of our economic system is that our money suffers from the repercussions of long-term inflation. We only have to think of the current price of essential goods which is eating away at our purchasing power.

In 1960, you needed 100 $ to eat for 3 months. Today, the same amount lasts only 3 days. This is why managing one's money must be better controlled.

Discipline and control, together with suitable budget planning, are the ingredients necessary to attain financial independence. I will broach this subject a little later on.

Everyone has an idea of how to manage their money better or how to set up a new business which can create collective prosperity and lead to financial independence. Make a list of your knowledge and abilities and take up the gauntlet.

Summary of Chapter 1

-   Believe in your own worth

- Search within yourself to discover what you can contribute to society

- The world always needs new ideas in order to progress

- Learn how to manage 100 $ before trying to manage 1 million $

- Find ways of becoming a true rich person

CHAPTER 2

Your Budget

Whether you are an employee or the owner of a business, you need to manage your money as appropriately as possible.

The word 'budget' conjures up an unpleasant daily task. I admit that it is difficult, but altogether achievable by ordinary people like you and me.

Writing down your expenses and keeping invoices requires a certain discipline, but it is a worthwhile undertaking because it is the best way of understanding exactly where your money goes on a weekly or monthly basis. The proof of this is that any serious business, whether it be a large multinational or a small company, keeps up-to-date records of expenditure and perfect accounting.

If you are loath to keep a note of your purchases on a daily basis, you can keep the invoices in a folder and deal with them monthly, either writing them down in a notebook or with the help of dedicated software. Like this, you will quickly be able to see your total monthly expenditure.

Drawing up a budget is a practical means of creating the habit of knowing where your money goes. After all, you work very hard to earn your living.

Financial pleasure can be interpreted as understanding what is happening to the money you earn each week and determining what you want to economize in the long term. If you intend to make some long-term capital, you need to know where you are starting from.

All financial specialists will agree that you should save at least 10 % of your annual income. Therefore, with a salary of $35,000, you need to put aside at least $3,500 per year. You will obviously find this difficult if you have never done so before.

If you find it hard to balance your budget, get into the habit of, first of all, collecting, and then paying, all your invoices. On the first day of the month, if you are unable to put the recommended 10 % of your monthly income into a special savings account, put just 2 %. The idea is to get things off the ground money likes action and movement. With the remainder, pay your bills. Do not be afraid of creditors. They will not cut off the phone straight away! You need to convince yourself in order to remove any fear of being short of money. Imagine that you have succeeded in putting $10,000 into the bank; why then would you not be capable of having $100,000 or even a million? If you believe you can do it, then nothing will stop you.

After several years of experience in the domain of financial services, I have gotten used to hearing people say that they are incapable of saving money each month. I believe that some of them experience poverty because they have never taken the trouble to regularly put a single dollar of their salary aside.

We have to create this new ritual in order to manage our money better. You are responsible for your financial happiness and no-one can replace you.

You may say it is ungrateful, but in the world of finance no-one will help you, whatever the goods you dream of acquiring. All human beings essentially need to retain their dignity in all circumstances. The government, itself in huge debt, cannot ensure the quality of life of its taxpayers in the future, unless there is a major turnaround of public finances.

If people never save, how can they get by? In my opinion, as soon as you are lucky enough to get a job, you should save at least a dollar a day. It is all a matter of choice and lifestyle.

Repeat the following motto in order to better apply it: "Don't spend more than your monthly income."

In short, establish what you need to live on, keep an eye on impulsive and nonessential buying, and fix your objectives for long-term investment even if it is only putting a small amount aside each week. At the end of the year, you will find that you have rapidly reached a thousand dollars, and without too much effort in the process.

Here are a few tips to help you save and to increase your prosperity:

- Whenever possible take advantage of bargain offers or second-hand goods. Certain objects can be almost as good as new.

- Buy a second-hand vehicle which has not done much mileage, for example a model that is two or three years old, and keep it as long as possible.

- Choose clothes which are classical in style and neutral in color. They will not go out of fashion and therefore serve you longer.

- Draw up a monthly plan for each of your expenses.

- Postpone nonessential purposes to a later date.

- Buy one item at a time and wait until you have the necessary funds before doing more shopping.

- Pay upfront. Make a list of what you need before going shopping and when you have finished go straight home.

- Rely on your reason and not your passion for all your purchases.

- Practice sports that do not cost anything, such as walking or cycling.

- Negotiate prices whenever possible, for example for car insurance, spare parts or second-hand objects.

- Turn off electric lights and turn down the heating in rooms that are not used very often in winter.

- Use your discount vouchers in shops that accept them. Do not buy groceries just before meals or if you are very hungry.

- Do home cooking. For instance, cook a turkey and serve part of it for one meal. Freeze the rest, which you will be able to use for future meals. Ready-made food becomes expensive after a while.

- Take advantage of after-season sales.

- Sell your odds and ends from time to time to make money from objects that you no longer use.

- Avoid taking out 'extra' insurance on your credit cards, they are usually poor quality and very expensive.

- Shop around to choose suitable financial institutions and keep an eye on the fees on your check account. There are reasonable accounts with small fees.

- Choose a credit card which does not include annual fees and settle the total monthly balance.

- Use all available discounts for intercity calls, and for your cell phone takes out the most practical and least expensive contract, depending on the amount of time you need for your calls.

- Travel out of season and take advantage of special offers during this period.

- Instead of buying new books, visit book fairs or go to the local library.

In short, use your talents and imagination to be as creative as possible. If you have a lot of friends, ask them if they have things that they no longer use. They will be only too happy to give them to you or sell them at a low price.

If you have time to meet with people in the financial domain or to read magazines on finance and investment, make the most of the opportunity. The more informed you are on the subject, the easier it will be for you to clarify your personal finances and budget.

Credit

Credit cards have endowed us with some kind of magic power, but which is very dangerous for the consumer. They allow us to obtain just about everything today, without any investigation of the credit involved. We live in an era of multi-colored plastic and the countless multimillionaire credit companies which do not hesitate to impose steep interest every month, even on their best customers.

Oil companies, department stores and the majority of financial institutions also offer laminated cards to use for purchases. And we receive offers by post urging us to take out easy loans which entice us to spend the totality of our pay.

What is unfortunate in all this is that these cards raise the ceiling of our credit and give us the impression that we are richer than we really are. In truth, when we go along with this practice we make ourselves poorer.

To prove this impoverishment, let us suppose that you wish to buy a new property or business. Your bank manager will ask you the amount of credit you have available. If you ignore this question, he will make an analysis of your credit file and tell you the whole truth about your financial situation. The upper limit to your credit will be considered by your bank manager as a total debt when he examines the qualifications of the loan you want to take out and your request will be refused.

In fact, the bank will probably refuse the loan because the ratio of your credit is too high as compared to your income, which means that that you will be in a dangerous situation if a new loan is granted and you will find it difficult to pay back the monthly installments.

You should never exceed a ratio of 38% between the total amount you spend each month and your income. See the example below:

You need to pay $425 a month for your car;

You are repaying a personal loan for the purchase of some furniture at $175 a month;

For $15,000 on your various credit cards, you pay 3 % a month, which equals a possible $450 for each monthly installment.

Thus your total monthly payments come to $1,050, which means that your total debt is too important, even supposing you to pay the balance of your credit card every month. Your bank manager will therefore consider that the total debt is too high since you exceed your debt ratio. Your income of $2,000 net per month is insufficient to cover the total debt even if your credit card is regularly paid each month.

Let me explain. We divide $1,025 by $2,000, which makes a ratio of 0:51. As mentioned above, the ratio should not exceed 0:38, so the bank will refuse the loan as the ratio is too high.

If you did not have a credit card, but only had to reimburse a loan for a car purchase at $225 a month, and you were happy to live with old furniture, your loan would probably have been accepted. But I understand your pride ... you don't want to drive an old jalopy or sit in a bucket, but sometimes the truth hits you hard. In the end it is the power of money which has the last word and not appearances.

We must rethink our way of managing how we spend our money. Indeed, we must stop letting ourselves be beguiled by the ease with which we can do it and by the various sections of financial banking which get richer and richer to the detriment of their clients.

Our ancestors were wiser than we are. They only bought things when they had the necessary money in their pockets to do so. It was perhaps slower to acquire goods in this way, but certainly safer in the long run.

I do not want to brand credit as being something harmful or totally outdated. I know very well how useful a credit card can be when one is travelling for example, but you must be able to refuse all the different cards that are offered and stop being financially dependent.

If you own a business, the scenario is completely different. Credit helps you to grow and to employ more personnel, as well as being a fiscal expense permitted by society.

N.B.: The examples above are hypothetical and should not be considered as being valid in reality. All depends on the policy of the bank and professional advisors. Check with your bank advisor for any question concerning the evaluation of your personal credit file.

Bad Debts and Good Debts

Examples of bad debts can be summed up as follows:

- Loans that you take out to buy goods which create no long-term value or which depreciate quickly. For example, a stereo system, a television or similar modern devices, a new motorbike, eating out at expensive restaurants or throw-away objects that can only be used once;

- When you buy luxury clothes that you only wear once and then leave them in your wardrobe for years;

- When you choose a new car which is not really necessary for getting around and that you only use now and then to travel 15 km between your house and your office. Moreover, you must take into account that it will lose at least 20 % of its value during the first year;

- All other purchases that do not put anything back into our pockets.

I appreciate that all these things embellish our way of life, but for our personal finances they are really harmful.

The main point to remember is that, in the long-term, these objects will lose their value instead of gaining any.

Let us now talk about *good debts*. These are the debts which will generate added value in the long-term and which will increase our personal assets. For example, taking out loans to:
- Buy pension schemes;

- Set up a business;

- Procure government bonds;

- Make investment funds;

- Buy property;

- Make improvements on a property;

- Invest in business;

- Anything that can assume greater value in the long term.

Eliminate Your Bad Debts

You should make a plan of how to reduce your bad debts. For example, if you have several credit cards, start off by paying the one which costs you the most interest. Each month, pay the highest amount possible in order to reduce the balance and only reimburse the minimum amount due on the other cards.

When you have completely paid off the amount due on one card, go on to deal with the next one and so on and so forth until you have nothing left to pay. Afterwards, cut up the most expensive cards and only keep one or two for convenience. In future, make sure you pay the total balance each month and carefully examine all your expenses.

A Plan for Prosperity in the Long Term

Once your debts have been paid, hurry up and set up an emergency fund representing three to six months of your salary.

Invest every week in a retirement pension scheme or in a sound area of investment. Go straight into action. Even if you only deposit 0.50 $ a day, it is not insignificant! Keep at it! Persevere and increase your deposits regularly whenever you can.

Once you have built up your emergency funds, invest in a more risky area such as a stock market mutual trust, a business or some other domain where you are sure that extra income will be generated in the long term. You must, first of all, be sure that the first two steps are really sound. Request information from professional financial advisors before taking any risks with your money. Knowledge is wisdom.

When you feel confident, start giving a certain percentage of your income each year to the charity or charities of your choice, fiscally recognized by the government. As well as helping the community, it will make you feel better. It also creates a space for accumulating even more prosperity through your creativity.

Your Balance Sheet

The balance sheet is neither more nor less than your real current net value. For example, if someone decides to make you a global proposal to buy all your assets, he will need to know exactly what you are worth on paper before making you a final offer.

For this it is necessary to take into account everything a person owns and subtract the debts in order to reach the net value. See the table below:

Hypothetical example: Julian's personal balance sheet

ASSETS
Cash account $2,000
Savings account $10,000
Retirement pension scheme $24,000
Real estate assets:
House $200,000

Chalet $33,000	
Other assets:	
Furniture $18,500	
Car $10,000	
Total assets $297,500	
LIABILITIES (Debts)	
Credit for car $5,000	
Mortgage $67,000	
Total liabilities $72,000	

Hence Julian's net value is:
($297,500$- 72,000) = $225,500

Or:
Total assets—Liabilities = Net value

A balance sheet is a good way to identify how much a person's assets are worth. By drawing up an annual balance sheet it is possible to estimate your financial situation and obtain an exact picture of what you actually have and what you owe to your creditors. As soon as you know the result, you can take any remedial actions that may be necessary.

Financial Advisors

Having worked in the world of finance for many years, I am proud to say that a financial advisor is very useful to help us weigh up our financial needs. Whether it is for planning our retirement, the management of a portfolio, invalidity or death, we can always benefit from his knowledge and good advice. It is never too late to think about forming a team of professionals: an accountant, a tax expert, a notary, an attorney and, of course, a financial advisor.

Request information from your business contacts to ascertain their competences. Most advisors will be eager to answer you, since it is their job, and some of them have very good knowledge of finance.

The advisor's role is to be a financial guide. He is not there to make everyday financial decisions for you. In any case there is no advisor or professional on whom you can rely on one hundred per cent. Start getting information about personal finances by attending seminars or by consulting financial journals. Choose trustworthy people with whom you get on well and confide personal information to them. Take decisive steps and do not be afraid to ask questions.

Hypothetical example of a budget plan (monthly simulation)

INCOME	
Net salary	$3,200
Other income	
Pension	
Annuities	
Total Income	$3,200
EXPENDITURE	
Fixed costs:	
Rent	$850
Electricity	$120

Insurance	$180
Telephone	$65
Cable TV	$40
Total fixed costs.	$1,255
Variable costs:	
(Food)	
Groceries	$700
Restaurants	$30
Total food	$730
(Transport)	
Fuel	$130
Car insurance	$50
Car maintenance	100 $
Total transport	$280
(Clothing)	$100
Cleaning	
Personal care	$100
Total personal	$200
(Vacation)	
Summer trip	$100
Total vacation	$100
(Health care)	$50
Medication	$50
Total health care	$100
(Miscellaneous)	

Donations to charity	$50	
Leisure activities	$100	
Total miscellaneous	$150	
Retirement savings	**$50**	
TOTAL EXPENDITURE	$2865	
Money remaining	$335	

This example may not apply to your own personal situation. However, it is important to be extremely vigilant and prudent with your spending since you have no doubt noticed that there are always more rows for expenses than there are for income. A thorough verification of your budget now and then will also help you to avoid disparities in your annual forecasts.

Having met many wealthy people, I know that impoverishment can happen to them too, because some of them do not keep accounts of what they spend.

In spite of their well-stocked bank accounts, they lack management and budget planning. They complain that everything costs more than it should do because they are unaware of where their money is really going.

Analyzing your personal transactions is essential to the creation of your long-term prosperity.

A source of Secondary Income to Start Investing

You often hear, "I don't have enough money to make investments..." If that is the case with you, there are two possible solutions:

1) Draw out from your budget resources a sum that you will keep strictly for savings

2) Restrict your expenses as much as possible and, if you cannot make ends meet, find an additional source of income.

A secondary income would be a wonderful formula for reimbursing your debts more rapidly and then being able to make investments. For example, an extra $200 a month would contribute to setting up an emergency fund and more long-term prosperity. If you already have a regular job, it is not impossible for you to devote some of your spare time to making some extra money.

Here are some suggestions for making money in your spare time:
- If you are a handyman, help other people to repair their houses in exchange for pay.

- Offer other businesses your assistance as a consultant in your domain of expertise.

- Become a conference speaker in your field of action.

- Launch a service for organizing weddings and other celebrations.

- Get involved in the sale of popular products (cars, computers).

- Set up a service for household maintenance.

- Start an internet marketing business, offering natural beauty products for example, and build up a network of people working for you.

- Offer your services for outdoor planning (gardens, terraces).

- Do accounting or secretarial work for companies.

- Become a marketing agent for businesses.

- Make good use of the time you spend on the internet taking advantage of companies which can help you make money online, or create your personal website.

- Propose your services as a painter/decorator.

- Make a business plan and sell it to a company (for example a brand or logo that stands out from others).

- Sell literary articles to magazines and newspapers.

- Give part-time private lessons.

- Open a nursery.

- Set up a grooming service for animals.

- Offer beauty treatment or massages.

- Become a part-time subcontractor for businesses or act as an independent management consultant.

- If you lack self-confidence, follow a course in your chosen field and launch a part-time business.

Financial Products

You will find below an overview of the most common financial vectors on the market. I will mention the type of products that the majority of people can obtain via the banking system, a broker or a brokerage firm, or a financial advisor who works for life insurance companies. Far be it from me to promote one or the other, however.

I only wish to explain the nature of all these vectors and what you can expect from each of them. The objective is to help you to discover ways of helping you to prosper. There is a large quantity of books on the subject, written by specialists that I would recommend you to consult in your local library.

You can never know enough about finance. Allow me to present the main lines.

Savings Accounts or Accounts With Operations Yielding Increasing Returns

In most cases these are accounts held in a financial institution. Nowadays most insurance companies also offer this service to their clients.

This type of account is very safe for your short-term projects, say for a period not exceeding three years. However it is not profitable to take this option on a long-term basis because of the low return of the interest rate. Moreover, high taxation makes it disadvantageous for the investor.

Government Bonds

This is a type of investment which usually yields short and long-term interest, commonly known as the coupon rate. The increase of the investment in the long term makes it appealing to the investor. The return is regular and the invested capital is safe. Bonds can be obtained from most banks or from investment brokers.

Treasury Bills

Treasury bills or T-bills constitute a short-term investment which procures a stable return and the means of generating a financial bolster for projects within five years. The government often needs this kind of short-term financing, and banks, as well as large businesses, use the liquidity provided by investors to support their activities, also in the short term. This type of liquid investment is very safe, while at the same time giving very reasonable long-term returns.

After issues, Treasury bills come to the payment date after 91 days, 101 days and 364 days. They can be obtained from a broker or from financial institutions and mutual funds companies. The bills can be issued by corporate security, governments or high quality private companies.

Term Deposit or Guaranteed Investment Contract

Banks usually propose this product to people for financing their loans and their credit activities. It is guaranteed and can often be bought back, but most of the time is linked to a fixed date, which allows its holder to renew it when it comes to expiry. The length of time varies from one to five years.

Over the last few years, financial institutions have created deposit certificates which are linked to the dividend yield from the stock exchange. Most of the time the return on the product is not guaranteed, unlike the capital which is guaranteed on the due date.

Stocks or Equity Securities

We are all able to become stockholders in a large company, such as Coca-Cola, and benefit in the long term from the latter's growth. On the other hand, as an owner or an investor, we take the risk of losing everything. We can make plenty of money, but we can also lose plenty of money, because our stocks are in just one company.

As long as coca sells well there is no problem, but if it does not, or if a manager makes some mistake you may well find yourself with big losses.

This non-guaranteed product, with variable return, fluctuates when there is an economic downturn or in time of war. Common stocks can fetch a dividend when the business is stable and making good revenues every year. Think in the long term in order to get a significant return. It is also wise to invest in several different companies at the same time via a mutual fund if you are new to this.

If you are willing to take risks and to study the principal of investing in the stock market in detail, stocks can be a good way of creating prosperity.

Preferred Stocks

Preferred stocks are different from common stocks in several ways. To sum up briefly, they are similar to bonds. Investors opt for preferred stocks because they are safe. Above all, they appreciate the dividend which represents a fixed return paid to their holders on a regular basis. Preferred stocks do not entail voting rights in the event of bankruptcy and give priority over holders of ordinary stocks in a company that does not protect the investor so well. This kind of stock is thus considered to be safer than common stock.

Mutual Funds

Investment funds, mutual funds or mutual investment funds—these three popular designations all refer to the same product. A mutual investment fund consists in grouping together several companies listed on the stock exchange and which are part of the same investment. For example, a government bond fund is made up of a large number of bonds issued by several companies. The investors' money is pooled and managed by a recognized financial institution.

The result is that purchasing power is higher and everything is managed by one or several financial professionals. Large banks or specialized institutions often promote this type of investment through their brokers or representatives of mutual investment funds.

Since they provide liquidity and are very varied, these funds offer great advantages which allow you to invest in a professional way in the majority of international markets. There are no management worries and the investments fluctuate less than in the case of a portfolio that a private investor can set up alone by negotiating directly via the internet.

Each fund is specialized. For instance, a mutual fund in natural resources will invest in mining companies, while others may only invest in banks or technology.

Purchasing is very simple. It is possible to open an account for only $25 a month or an annual deposit of $500. The risk is low and on the whole the funds follow the index of major North American stock markets. It is preferable to start off with a mutual investment fund since it is less unpredictable. You should remember that when you invest, you should consider the long-term, at least a ten-year period. From experience, I know that people often tend to be impatient and hope to make big profits quickly, but unfortunately this miracle will not happen, whatever kind of investment you choose to make.

The logic behind the long-term investment is to beat inflation or at least to maintain our cost of living. If our investments regularly yielded an amazing 30% profit each year, nobody would be able to change their car or renovate their kitchen because costs would be so blown up by inflation in the economy and would lead to exponential development of the stock market. It is preferable to have rises and falls in the market in order to guarantee a certain equilibrium in the global economy.

Historically speaking, mutual funds became very popular in the 1980s, at a time when there were very few gamblers in the market. With time, together with greater technological possibilities, investors have become better informed, so that nowadays most financial institutions offer their own family of mutual funds.

Having become more democratic over time, it is easy to obtain a new mutual fund with an institution or bank. The main problem is to find a competent administrator to manage all this money and to invest according to the wishes of the consumer from one year to another. The manager of a mutual fund must be experienced, stable and reliable, able to stay in his position within the same company for a long time in order to succeed in getting good returns. As a result, it is important to vary your investments with good explanations from an advisor.

The industry of mutual funds is now very competitive and it is time to hire better managers. So beware of funds that are in the spotlight and which boast returns exceeding 30% for a given year. Frequently this wonderful dividend disappears into thin air the following year because the star manager has left his job to join another company which has more to offer him.

It is therefore necessary to know our personal tolerance to risk and to build up a balanced portfolio made up of mutual funds, bonds, good quality common stocks and preferred stocks. It is imperative to study one's own finances carefully before investing in a fund.

With time and experience, I have found that not everybody is comfortable with risk. Your investments should never keep you awake at night. We all work very hard to save a few dollars every month and it is obvious that we do not wish to lose anything.

Types of Funds on The Market

a) Money Market Funds

Money market funds use money market tools such as Treasury bills, government papers or loan papers from large companies. They procure revenues, liquidity, and secure your capital during the investment period. The dividends will vary according to the interest paid on the investments.

This kind of investment ensures minimum risk, easy liquidity and almost no long-term instability.

b) Mortgage Funds

Mortgage funds buy credit on residential and commercial mortgages. Dividends will vary according to the revenues generated on the mortgages and the possibilities of earning capital by selling equity.

As a general rule, mortgage funds are low risk, but since long-term return is not very high it is better to invest on a short-term basis.

c) Bond or Revenue Funds

Bond funds buy bonds from the government or from large commercial companies, either open or closed. The return varies according to the income from the interest on the bonds and the capital profit obtained by the managers.

The risk is minimal in the medium term, depending on the type of bond issued by the company. Economic or governmental factors, variation in the interest rate, inflation and the quality of management can greatly affect the variation of the return.

d) Dividend Funds

These funds provide revenues directly from the financial viability of the business, through high-quality common and preferred stocks. They are advantageous on a fiscal level and in the long-term offer the possibility of capital profit. The risk is average.

e) Balanced Funds

Balanced funds, which can be considered to have a normal cruising speed in the world of investment, aim for a certain security for capital and a balance between revenues and added value from stocks. With an average risk, they have the advantage of increasing substantially in the long term.

These funds have a mixture of components—usually a significant proportion of stocks invested in large companies together with bonds, which yield a constant revenue in the long term. *They allow the investor to get off to a good start in the world of investment.*

f) Stock Funds

Stocks constitute a higher risk and require more complex management.

Stock or equity funds aim for an increase of capital in the long term, by buying stocks from small, medium-sized and large companies. Sometimes these funds buy small, growing businesses and this makes them more unpredictable and thus more difficult for the investors.

The profit from these funds is very interesting if people are ready to live with the ups and downs of the market. Several economic and geopolitical factors can affect the return in the space of a decade.

g) International Funds

International funds run from average to very high risk depending on individual objectives. If we keep them on a long-term basis, they can, however, prove to be very interesting. The problem lies with the administrators who try and identify the countries which have good potential for economic growth. Political situations and the fluctuations in foreign currencies can affect the return in the long term and create added complications.

h) Specialized Funds

Specialized funds concentrate their investment in a given sector, such as a developing economic region or a specific category of company. They might therefore buy only stocks from banks or mining companies, for example.

These are consequently not recommended for the majority of people for investment.

i) Private Management Funds

Certain types of investment for privileged people are available on the market. The amount to pay in order to enter this niche is usually around $100,000 or more.

It is important to be aware that this strategy requires the investor's knowledge of the kind of assets that make up this type of investment.

Likewise, the manager in charge of the funds must be competent and have an impeccable record in the domain of management and prove that in the past he has had exceptional returns.

It is recommended making a thorough study before investing such a large amount of money.

The disadvantage of investing in such schemes is the danger that the private manager discontinues his activity due to change of career or retirement.

As his successor is unknown, this may cause problems for future return. The firm must have a team of competent administrators to ensure that it stays on course and provides security to investors for their capital.

These firms usually have a high standard of regulations with the financial authorities, ensuring that investors are properly protected.

Nevertheless, this does not guarantee the security on either return or the capital. You should never put more than 10% of your personal fortune in this kind of investment.

j) Ethical Funds

Ethical funds invest in "clean" businesses. They will not, for instance, approach companies that pollute the environment or produce waste products that are dangerous to people's health.

Now that you have a general idea about investment funds it is up to you to choose those which, according to your personality, suit you best.

To conclude on the subject of mutual funds:

Since diversification is the key to success, it is essential to ensure that you vary your investments by only devoting a certain percentage of your financial assets to each financial vector.

Diversification also means investing the world over and not just in one particular country with a single category of assets such as stocks or bonds.

Take advantage of all the products that exist on the market. Request information from your financial advisor. Look for objective information that can really guide you, taking into account your risk tolerance.

Investment is an active process. Our system for increasing personal wealth is created through time and experience.

Do not delay in investing a few dollars in dedicated seminars or books that deal with finance and planning. This will be beneficial to you on all levels.

Summary of chapter 2

- Study each of your investments

- Ask questions

- Read books on the subject of finance

- Listen to radio programs

CHAPTER 3

Your Financial Protection

We all have at heart to earn our living and do all we can to improve our financial situation. Unfortunately—or fortunately—there comes a day when we have to retire and yet continue to live well.

In the meantime, we run the risk of falling ill, or dying, or being pursued by creditors after death. I want to make you aware of the importance of making sure our investments are safe.

When we plan our life, we often wait until the last minute before making proper arrangements.   When we die, we leave our family behind us. For dignity's sake, we do not wish to leave our near and dear ones to run the risk of poverty.

The following paragraphs will help you to understand the financial language and the various programs for ensuring our financial security.

Life Insurance

You may perhaps have already experienced a death in your family or know someone who has had an accident or died suddenly, leaving their family bereaved. Hence we must protect ourselves because no-one is shielded from these sad events. As for the fact of dying one day, we are not talking about risk but with certainty.

People say that they are over-insured, but what happens when the person in charge of the family suddenly disappears? Take the example of a 39 year-old father who dies, leaving behind him a wife and three children. With insurance amounting to only $25,000, how will his widow meet the needs of her family?

One solution could be to apply for a well-paid job, depending, of course, on her competences and experience. She could also try and find a new, comfortably off partner, but nothing can guarantee that she will succeed.

As it is sometimes difficult to find a job nowadays, particularly when one has little training, she should perhaps contact the government to find out what means they can give her to subsist. This is the second, and worst, solution!
The last attempt, if she cannot find another solution, is to sell all her possessions and try to live on the proceeds for as long as possible. Living in a flat, she will have to live from hand to mouth and, sooner or later, look for another source of income to compensate for the deficiency.

People may have a lot of insurance, but will this protection be adequate in case of necessity?

Many people believe that they are safe thanks to their insurance against accidents, but do not realize that most of the time the latter only work in the event of death in a car, plane or bus. It is more than likely that they are not insured for a natural death, which is after all the first cause of mortality.

You must not wait to protect yourself, particularly if you have a family. Don't forget that $500,000 insurance yields a revenue of $25,000 for life, corresponding to 5% interest. Your beneficiary will then be able to solve any financial problems and avoid social and economic headaches for their family.

Life insurance policies can also serve as a cover when you take out a loan to buy a business or property with a financial institution. Most of the time the latter will demand this cover as warranty in the event of your sudden demise, in order to easily reimburse the loan in question.

Furthermore, when you are in business, insurance is very useful to cover your associates. If one of your best associates should die, how will you cope during the 300 days following his decease?

From a fiscal point of view, the best planning tool remains life insurance, since death benefits are not liable to tax. It enables one to settle one's estate, either personal or business, to pay any other taxes owing to the government.

Some single people hesitate to take out insurance because they have no children. In this case it is useful to remember that they may still have a family left behind: parents, brothers or sisters. Frequently the latter need liquidity to settle debts, not to mention probable expenses following the death and the taxes on the deceased's possessions.

The advantage of life insurance is that it is cannot be seized by creditors when a personal beneficiary such as a close relation is mentioned in the contract. When a beneficiary is designated, it is always preferable to add that the contract is liable to annulment rather than irrevocable in order to avoid complications.

Types of Life Insurance

To what type of insurance should one subscribe? Sometimes it is a question of personal choice.

A life insurance policy has guaranteed premiums for the entire length of the contract, that is to say up until your death. After a certain number of years, it is possible to free the policy, meaning that you no longer pay the premiums but nevertheless remain insured for a predetermined capital established at the date of the subscription. In fact these are the surrender values (values from savings linked to the contract) which are not bought back and which pay your premium. The day you decide to recover your surrender values, your policy is canceled.

With this type of contract, it is a good idea to check how much your current surrender values are worth as well as the paid-up capital, for the sake of organizing your personal finances.

As you have probably guessed, this type of policy is more expensive than the second sort, which is the temporary policy. The latter has no surrender values and cannot be freed of premium payments after a certain number of years.

Financial products have developed over the years and it is now possible to obtain a contract paid in ten years for an entire life policy. This option is very interesting in that it avoids paying insurance all our lives.

The third and last type of insurance, which arrived on the market in the 1980s, is the universal life insurance. This policy is partly insurance and partly savings, the latter consisting in a scheme which enables both protection and the possibility of accumulating money which is not liable to tax.

Compared to the other types of insurance, universal life insurance is more flexible since as well as being able to put a lot of money into it, it is also possible to withdraw money. This excellent vector of investment enables the policy holder to opt for higher payments when he so desires. To avoid the policy quickly declining, it is necessary to cover the minimum amount required in the contract.

A business owner will find this very useful as it enables him to put money into savings, while at the same time protecting his assets. Thus it is possible to nominate an irrevocable beneficiary, such as one's partner or child, thereby making it impossible to seize the policy in the event of bankruptcy or prosecution.

One of the advantages of the universal life policy is that it can accumulate sums of money to build up an appreciable retirement fund and increase death benefits. The latter ensure that taxes can be paid and the family can thrive.

This policy is an excellent choice if one is prepared to invest significant amounts over a long period.

It will ensure that the taxes as well as our final expenses are paid after our demise, without leaving any debts for others to pay.

It is important to choose the right vector according to the situation. For many, paying insurance premiums is not something particularly amusing.

Let us go back to the temporary policies. These are mostly subjected to a fixed period of 10 or 20 years. After that they can be renewed with premiums adapted according to your age at the time. This is the biggest disadvantage, because when you have reached 60 your premium will have become more expensive and you may no longer be able to pay it unless you have put enough money aside to benefit from it up until the end of the contract.

A temporary insurance policy is the most affordable and hence very interesting for young couples with children or people with a low income. The transformation provision which is guaranteed with this plan gives you the possibility to convert your temporary policy into a permanent one, with a fixed premium for the rest of your life.

It is preferable not to wait until too late in life before deciding to convert your temporary policy into a permanent one, since the cost will be calculated according to your age when you do so.

To sum up, the advantage of having life insurance is the creation of a significant estate which can meet the needs of your family. Envisaging death is never joyful, but as it is something that we all come to one day it is better to foresee the consequences.

Disability Insurance

Disability insurance is a safeguard of riches, that is to say of our revenues.

Like the majority of people who work we are convinced that disability only happens to other people and never to us. However, according to statistics, one person in three runs the risk of becoming disabled before the age of 65.

You must plan out your income. What would your income be in the event of disability? One person might reply, "I have some money in the bank if ever that should happen." It remains to be seen whether the amount would be adequate to maintain the same pace of life. Not many people manage to put aside a month's salary in the bank as a safeguard for such a contingency.

Another person might say, "I have absolutely nothing." A self-employed person no doubt works very hard and does not always have time to think about taking care of these financial details.

Others again still believe that the government will be there to help them in the event of disability. But it can often be seen, you need to battle against a lot of administrative and legal red tape before succeeding in getting any benefits from government bodies.

Employees of large companies contribute, along with their employers, to a collective insurance scheme, which ensures adequate protection in case of disability.

From experience, I would recommend allocating 3% to 5% of your income to a disability insurance scheme. This will ensure good protection since you will find numerous products in this domain on the market.

People always surprise me with their notion that paying insurance to protect their salary is expensive, while at the same time they admit to insuring their car, their house or their boat. As a financial advisor, I ask them if their salary is not more important to their well-being than insuring their stereo system against theft. I point out that allocating $100 a month to be able to cope with possible disability is perhaps a more judicious outlay.

Private disability insurance is available via many companies. The benefits are usually not liable to tax, since we pay for them with money that we have earned and that has already been taxed.

Here are a few questions that you should ask yourself before signing an insurance contract:

- For how long will the benefits are paid to me? One year, five years, ten years or when I reach the age of 65?

- If I become disabled this morning, how long will I have to wait before receiving the benefits? One month, four months or a year?

- Will I be covered for partial disability?

- What is not included in the contract? Will the benefits be limited to my back problems, for example a hernia or lower back strain?

Serious Illnesses

A new type of insurance has existed for several decades now owing to the large number of heart attacks and forms of cancer. If we succumb to such illnesses, companies offer the possibility of financial indemnity. For example, if you have suffered a heart attack and after six months you are completely recovered, you could benefit from $100,000. You will not get a new heart, but at least you will be in a better financial position, since illness and loss of time lead to significant expenses and you do not know in what condition you will be when you go back to work.

It is possible to be insured for a minimum of $25,000. Moreover, most companies offer to reimburse the premium after a certain length of time and at death. This means that you only loser the interest that you would in any case not have received if you had invested your money in some other way.

It is in our interest to understand the importance of this product when planning out our lives, as we all know, people who have experienced heart problems or cancer.

When illness comes and wipes out our projects or casts a shadow on our retirement, we no longer wonder whether $50,000 is useful in such events.

Even if money does not bring happiness, it can nevertheless help us to get through ordeals and pay our medical bills.

Property Insurance

You have one or several cars, plus furniture that you need to protect from fire, theft or water damage. Read your insurance contracts for your house and furniture from time to time to check that you are covered for floods and major catastrophes.

Ensure that as many provisions as possible are included in the guarantee since catastrophes can occur unexpectedly at any time. Some, often quite cheap, insurance can save you a great deal of money.

Do not wait for a catastrophe to happen before calling your broker. Talk to him about the guarantees included in your contract. The information you find concerning your house and furniture may very well surprise you.

Take photos and make a list of your possessions and put all this in a safe place in case of fire. In this way you will be able to give proof of your real values if asked to do so.

Do not be afraid of asking for information to understand the principles of insurance. As there are often many provisions in a contract, ask for explanations about the most important ones to understand.

The Will and Testament

A will is a privileged document containing all the provisions for the transmission of your goods when you die. It can be modified at any time.

There are several kinds of will:

a) The Holographic Will

The holographic will is entirely handwritten and signed by the testator. It is valid as such without any formality or witness. However, at the testator's death, it must be certified by a court. Divergence of interpretation may cause problems as to the distribution of goods to the heirs.

The advantage of the holographic will is that there are no costs involved in drawing it up.

b) The Witnessed Will

The witnessed will be written by the testator by hand or word processed. It requires two witnesses, neither of whom must know, at the testator's decease, the latter's desires or what he has written. Like the holographic will, it must be approved by a court at the testator's death.

It is now possible to obtain preprinted examples of wills which can be filled out by the testator. However, if it is not properly completed, this may lead to problems when the testator dies.

c) The Certified Will

The certified will is the best option since it is drawn up before a legal professional, either a notary or an attorney, depending on where you live. The fact that it is certified simplifies the liquidation and facilitates the administration aspects linked to death. Furthermore, in Quebec, it is registered with the chamber of notaries, which offers greater security. It clearly specifies the role of the liquidator, that is to say the person who has been nominated to administer your succession after death. Do not hesitate to consult a good accountant or tax specialist to establish the list of your valuables.

We do not know what is going to happen to our possessions after our demise and I believe that we should be well informed about the impact of death. Nobody would like to learn that their goods have been liquidated only a few hours after their death.

A will is an instrument or guide which will work on your behalf after your death by clearly enumerating your wishes.

It is not only a legal document with which you give your possessions to such and such a person. It is much more. It is the written proof of your decisions and wishes.

Trusts

A trust is a financial tool which enables the good management of your possessions after your decease. It is an entity in its own right and distinct from the individual people who constitute it.

A trust mentions the name of the person who will administer the money and who will benefit from its revenues. For example, if you have a handicapped child, he will not be able to look after your affairs after your death, but a trust can do it for him. A financial institution specialized in inheritance administration can sometimes act as a trust.

Some of the advantages of trusts are:

- They can help with the inheritance of your business.

- They offer financial advantages to someone who is dear to you, such as a spouse or partner, for as long as they live.

- They protect your financial assets from creditors.

- They protect important possessions such as valuable paintings.

- They offer financial protection for your children (education, clothing, food).

- They provide better management of family fortunes.

- They can manage your property.

It is even possible to set up social trusts which pay the amount of money into cultural, religious, scientific, educational or philanthropic organizations. This kind of trust does not aim to make a profit, but rather a moral or spiritual interest by preserving wealth in society. Its objective is to preserve your accumulated riches.

It is a good idea to request information and advice about trusts since there are many different options that can be adapted to your personal situation.

The Mandate in Case of Incapacity

Like the will, the mandate in case of incapacity is useful when your health declines following an illness or accident. This document will protect you and enable the efficient administration of your possessions by a designated person, the agent, who will act as moral and physical manager of all your assets and ensure your physical security. It is consequently important to choose a competent person on whom you can rely.

Example of a Couple: Anne and Patrick

Anne and Patrick both have a job. Each of them has a car and they have two properties, one of which is the lovely house in town where they live. They have three children.

Patrick and Anne do not agree about their personal finances. They have unpaid credit cards and are behind in reimbursing certain loans. They would like to save money, but Anne and Patrick like spending, and since they often refill their credit cards their accounts are far from brilliant. As they have a high mortgage, they cannot really indulge in such extravagance.

The children also ask a lot of their parents, and the latter have to say no. As a result, the family situation sometimes becomes strained. In fact, they are not really sure how their finances have come to this state.

Their situation has become intolerable and they have to do something to solve their financial problems. They are proud and like to keep up appearances—they own a boat and a motorbike as well as their two recent cars.

As an IT expert, Patrick earns $65,000 per annum, whilst Anne earns $30,000 as a secretary. They have a lot of expenses and there is nothing left at the end of the month. Even if they manage to pay everything, they still often end up with an average deficit of $500 a month. If they do not both commit to simplifying their way of life, they will find it difficult to get by.

After discussion, the couple decides to meet with a financial advisor and draw up a budget. During this meeting, Anne and Patrick realize that spending money in certain areas does not yield any profit and does not generate any revenue for their retirement. They are creating no long-term prosperity. They consequently draw up a five-year plan in order to reduce their debts and they begin to save $150 a month to build up an emergency fund equivalent to three to six months' income.

This initial step makes them conscious of the grim reality of their daily consumption habits. The couple must review their objectives together so as to follow the development of their consumption and they must do this every month in order to avoid conflict. They need to love one another more deeply to build a better future.

After three years they have finished reimbursing their consumer debts and sold some of the non-essential goods such as the chalet and the boat. They have found this ordeal enriching in spite of certain disappointments.

Feeling happier now, they have learned how to control their spending and they start investing in a retirement pension scheme and they have even grown to enjoy these new habits.

They become more interested in everything to do with finance by reading newspapers and they regularly follow their financial portfolio. Furthermore, they have the pleasant surprise each month of finding that they have a surplus $500 in their budget.

The net family value on their balance sheet has gone from $2,000 to $90,000 in the space of 5 years. Now they have no more debts, their ambition is to reach the amount of $150,000 in the next few years.

Over the past five years, Patrick has set up an IT business with a friend. His income has consequently increased by about $1,000 a month. As for Anne, she enjoys attending seminars on finance and investment and her understanding of money matters has become more acute with time.

Anne and Patrick continue to keep an eye on their personal spending even if their financial situation a whole lot healthier than it was. They want to stay free and therefore avoid getting tied up with material things. They agree to live more modestly and to make donations to charities. They now use their goods longer, thereby preserving the planet from industrial pollution.

Summary of the three chapters

- Prosperity is to be found within us, with our beliefs and thoughts, and not externally.

- Transform your way of life into a mode of saving and increasing your wealth.

- Always seek out new knowledge.

- Check your net value and your expenses every 6 months.

- Draw up a monthly budget and follow up on all your invoices.

PERSONAL NOTES

Chapter 4

Wise Ideas

For your financial projects, always think in the long term. The short term is sometimes bad counsel.

You are responsible for all your financial decisions so you must master your personal finances and also the business world if you are self-employed.

Always negotiate important purchases.

If you buy equity on the stock market, make sure you are aware of the financial resources of the business in question from its balance sheet and financial results. Above all, find out who the directors of the company are.

Take a look at the salaries and see if these are in line with the company's financial capacity.

We have seen many companies close down because the directors were too greedy with their own remuneration.

The best opportunities arise in finance when everyone is afraid of major recession.

Make friends with your advisor and ask him plenty of questions. If he does not have all the answers, call another advisor. You can never have enough advice before acting.

Use all legal possibilities to reduce your taxes, such as tax shelters and investment in your own company.

When you save tax on your revenues, you can increase your wealth by buying additional assets in the company in order for it to flourish and generate more jobs.

When you launch a business, write down a clear and simple vision of what you would like it to become in time and present your forecast of the revenues to your bank manager and private lender.

Foreign investments such as mutual or property funds entail a lot of risk, so do not invest large sums of money on the pretext that someone told you it was lucrative.

There are often negative circumstances, such as the fluctuation of foreign currencies and geopolitical situations leading to extra taxation. Consult experts who live in the country in question.

If you are 50 years old or more, you should never invest more than 50% of your portfolio in stocks in order to avoid a catastrophe if the market collapses.

The ideal situation is to have 3 different kinds of investments – 40% to 50% for security, in bonds for instance, 35% for moderate growth, like dividends, and lastly, 10% to 15% in a riskier sector, such as in a high-quality business with good prospects of growth over time. In this way your investments will be balanced at any given time.

Make sure that you keep track of this distribution on a regular basis in order to avoid a significant decrease of your values.

Chapter 5

- *How to Cure Your Relationship with Money*

1. - *Money represents positive creative energy which can help humanity*

Having a good deal of money will allow you to elaborate specific projects to realize your dreams and the dreams of your family.

Money offers the possibility of having more happiness and self-confidence and contributes to self-fulfillment.

When you think of money, associate it with a feeling of joy and gratitude and it will come into your life.

When you think of money you should always keep in mind the idea of prosperity, and never an idea of shortage. Always think that money will be there to help you at the right time.

Have an image of surplus in your mind and wait patiently for the universe to reward you abundantly.

Visualize money coming from all quarters and that you are going to attract it in many different ways, even when you are asleep.

If you believe that money is an energy of love, then you will feel good as soon as you think about it.

Put love into your bank and wallet along with your money. Respect the money that you have.

Imagine that God exists and that he gives you the responsibility of managing what you already have and what you will receive. Suppose that everything belongs to God, including banknotes. Our role is to become a good manager in life.

2- *Stop Judgment

When you think that someone has more dollars than you, do not be offended. It is as if you are sending a message to the universe saying, "I don't like money and I don't need it because I hate people who have more than I do." Judgment cuts off the physical and creative energy needed to attract prosperity.

Bless those who have more money than you do and imagine that they get even more and that they will use it to help other people and offer solutions to humanity as a whole.

Avoid being critical about money. If someone that you know has a nice car, compliment him on it and do not expect anything in return.

Avoid all feelings of jealousy towards friends or relations who have more than you. Appreciate people for what they are and not for what they have, and do not think of money before everything else. Be nice to people because everyone possesses a beautiful heart and soul.

3- *The dangers of internal and external dialogue

When you say to yourself, "I don't have enough money," you make it even more likely to be true and you will end up ruined and unable to believe in life's bounty. The world becomes hostile and cold because you are convinced that nothing is possible for you.

You should program your subconscious with a choice of words that illustrate prosperity. For example, say to yourself that you deserve more, that you are a good and talented person and that your affairs are getting better and better each day, and you will find that you attract money easily.

When you have good communication with other people, avoid saying things like, "times are hard" or "we have to tighten our belts". Your self-esteem and your individual worth will only grow if you are prudent about your inner dialogue.

As soon as you start thinking about money, immediately start a positive dialogue with yourself and think of nothing else but the affluence that is going to arrive in your life like a river full of banknotes. You are always free to choose your thoughts and language concerning prosperity.

4- *The Magic of Thinking Big

Imagine that you already have everything that you want.

For example, you dream of having a million dollars; it is not only pleasant but praiseworthy to think like this. There is nothing better than thinking and acting as though you already had this money in your possession.

People's thoughts are more powerful than you may suppose. By acting like someone who has a million dollars, you act with confidence and in security.

You will notice that all your actions are inspired by a new strength within you. And every business transaction that you carry out will prove to be profitable in the long term.

Your current way of thinking will become the driving force for obtaining what you want in life. You must be careful about the thoughts you send to the universe because they return even more powerfully, due to the law of attraction.

5- *The Free Circulation of Money

Be careful to pay your invoices as rapidly as possible.

When you receive an invoice for a credit card, be quick to pay the balance of your account for the sake of your peace of mind.

Invoices that mount up are a way of fleeing prosperity in your mind because you always have the idea that you are going to be short of money.

Therefore, as soon as you have the possibility, take pleasure in paying, and always pay a little more than the required minimum amount.

In this way you send a message of prosperity to the universe and the universe will help you.

Do not be afraid of rapidly paying all your debts to your creditors, for this is how you can prove to yourself that you always have money flowing freely into your life.

6 - *Put an end to your doubts about money and heal the past

Be aware of all the thoughts you have about money that are related to your past. If you have been traumatized about money since childhood, say to yourself that you want to be freed from your financial past.

Find a sentence that you will repeat over and over again when necessary, such   "I am open to receiving new energy about money with love and gratitude and I welcome it as a beautiful light coming into my life."

7- *Think about your dreams and your vision

People who are rich today do not always get excited about the money factor before beginning their desire for it. Before getting rich they had dreams—for example, Disney thought about how he could attract people to an amusement park. Afterwards, he looked for financial backers to sponsor his project and, finally, he found a partner to help him realize it. If he had counted too much on money before starting off, he would have achieved nothing in life because he would have wasted too much energy worrying about the shortage of banknotes.

It is essential to establish an accurate vision of what we want to attain in our lives and to enjoy the work necessary towards making our project come true. Money often comes more quickly as a result, without having to force it.

One of the best pieces of advice is to put love into everything that you want to do and money will follow. Many millionaires often make the following assertion: pinpoint your passions and in time you will find how to make your activities profitable.

8- *See Opportunities

Life is a continual opportunity. When you look at activities as being a source of prosperity, then you are opening up your thoughts towards development.

When I visit downtown New York or Toronto, I see all the affluence that exists in our lives. There are the great buildings of the insurance companies and magnificent banks and I say to myself that there is certainly a lot of prosperity for me in life.

Look at every problem in society as an opportunity for your finances. If you can discover a new service or product that can solve a problem in the world, then you can open the doors to prosperity for yourself too. Just be creative every day and you will build yourself a wonderful life. Ask yourself the question: how can I help humanity on this new day that life has offered me?

9—* Life Without Boundaries

Why should we put boundaries on our lives? Do not put a financial ceiling on your life. When you think about your retirement pension, imagine that it is so large that every year you will be able to give money to worthy causes or charities.

If you are starting up a business, again do not put a financial limit on it. Plan it so that revenues and profits can grow every year in an exponential way.

Continually think profit and keep your expenditure under control. Give more added value to society and to your clients.

If you are an employer, offer a retirement pension scheme to your employees so that they can get richer while working for you.

10 - *Being rich is 80% psychological and 20% mechanical

It is your attitude that builds up your wealth, not just your financial strategies and mechanisms. If you see yourself as a millionaire, you are more likely to become one than if you are forever thinking about the ways of becoming one.

Why is it that some people who have lost all their money are capable of bouncing back again in just a few years? The response is simple— they said to themselves: if I had this wealth before, I can build it up again.

They have a millionaire's attitude, their financial thermostat is plugged into millions and they have no doubts in their minds. The American billionaire Donald Trump is an example of this. At a certain time in his life he lost almost everything and yet he has romped home to rebuild his fortune. It is his attitude which made him say to himself, "I can start over and bounce back."

When I heard a statement by Anthony Robbins during a seminar, it immediately altered my relationship with money and helped me to move forward. He said, "When everything is going badly with your finances, ask yourself if you have the attitude of a millionaire or a pauper."

Take care of your psychology by listening to rich people or by reading books about prosperity. This is the best path to take towards your own financial success.

11 - *Rise Above Financial Stress

Start writing a diary and mention your gratitude for your relationship with money. If you have access to the internet and there is a free seminar about money by an author or conference speaker, say thank you to life.

If you find a coin on the ground, take the time to thank life.

If someone wishes you prosperity, write it down in your diary in the evening and thank the person in question.

Be an inspector of gratitude. Every time you receive a free product or service, write it down and appreciate the generosity of the universe.

First and foremost, respect yourself and take the time to like yourself because you deserve it. In respecting yourself more and considering yourself a nice person, you will be able to have more respect for the money that comes in and out of your life.

Life joyfully and appreciate your life, while not diverging from your gratitude for everything.

Be proud of yourself, no matter how much money you have. It is not what you have now that counts but how you treat your own person.

Dare to be what you want to be and act as if everything were already in place. If you think like a millionaire, you have a good chance of being more and having more in your life.

The sky is your limit. Look at the myriad stars in the heavens and imagine that your fortune is as large as the number of stars.

Confidence in life and in yourself is fundamental. If you have faith in what you do, you will feel the same about money.

Dare to rise above financial fears. Sometimes you need to spend a lot of money to do a lot of things and the best way is to feel comfortable with the comings and goings of money.

It is essential to like yourself and other people. When you really like yourself it is also a message that you send directly to God: "I deserve more because I give more love."

12-* More Action Is Necessary

It is all very well to imagine that you have 10 million dollars in the bank and to visualize it, but if you do not take any action, nothing will happen in concrete terms.

Action is necessary on a daily basis; you need to create a sort of ritual of success. Successful people are like you, no more, no less, and we are all equal. They eat three times a day and go to bed every evening. They have a positive attitude and make small steps every day towards their dreams and vision. This is what makes the difference between them and the rest of the population.

Ritual is necessary in your lives. The most beautiful castles are built of stone by stone, every day.

There are always solutions to solve your financial problems if you believe and persist.

13- *Ask Often

To have money, you must ask for it. For example, if you want $10,000, you should consider where you could offer a service that would bring in the equivalent sum.

You owe it to yourself to regularly request things from people. If you want to buy goods, ask for a discount so that you make some savings and, with the same principle, get richer.

Do not be embarrassed to ask as often as possible and whenever the opportunity arises. If you are in a restaurant, ask for more fries! Ask for more remuneration when you offer people good customer service with your business.

As soon as you can, ask for a salary rise and if your employer does not give you a positive response, then go and find a new employer who offers better conditions and who will accept your request.

The choice is yours and you are always free to demand more from life.

14- *Add Value

Add value to people's lives without necessarily immediately asking for something in return. For instance, if you are starting up a business, nothing stops you from offering a better service than the majority of your competitors.

This may seem difficult at the beginning, but it is what will make your business different from the others and give you the edge.

Added value is necessary because most people are not prepared to go the extra mile. If you communicate and give more to people, the result will be that you will get money and also improve your relationship with money by not sparing yourself and giving wholeheartedly.

15-* The Feeling of Permanent Prosperity

You are an energetic person and every second you produce from deep inside you a thought which is creative for your destiny. This thought will give you a precise answer with time.

If you are currently living in poverty, there is nothing to stop you from starting to experience within you a powerful feeling of prosperity. Play the part of a film star who acts and thinks as though he has a fortune.

Imagine that you travel in the best planes and sleep in the finest hotels on earth and eat in first-class restaurants.

Think that the horn of plenty is for you rather than the dry crust of poverty.

A feeling of prosperity is also a question of self-respect. It sends a clear message to the universe and its energy that you were born to be rich and nothing less.

Smile at people whenever you have the opportunity and wish them all the best in their lives in every domain. Each and every one of us deserves happiness, health and prosperity in order to pay our bills and receive that extra bounty from the heavens.

Worksheet

Exercise

Set down clearly what you want to obtain from life.

What are your financial objectives in the short and long term?
1 —

_____

_____

_____

_____

2 —_____

_____

_____

_____

3 —_____

_____

_____

_____

4 —_____

_____

_____

_____

What are your personal and family objectives? :
1 —_____

_____

_____

2 —_____

3 —

4 —

How would you define your mission in life?

1 —

2 —

3 —

4 —

Material Objectives

What possessions would you like to have in life?

1 —

_____

_____

_____

_____

2 —

_____

_____

_____

3 —

_____

_____

_____

4 —

_____

_____

_____

_____

What would be the best way of serving humanity?
1 —

_____

_____

_____

2 —
_____
_____
_____
_____

3 —
_____
_____
_____
_____

4 —
_____
_____
_____
_____

What is your idea of perfect life?

1 —
_____
_____
_____
_____

2 —
_____
_____
_____
_____

3 —
_____
_____
_____
_____

4 —

_____

_____

_____

_____

Training

What would be the best training for you to increase your worth on the market?

1 —

_____

_____

_____

_____

2 —

_____

_____

_____

_____

3 —

_____

_____

_____

_____

4 —

_____

_____

_____

_____

Thank you for reading.

About the author.

Marc Thériault is the author of 7 books:
Croire en soi (*Believing in oneself*) 2005
100 Jours de chance (*100 days of luck*) 2007
100 Jours de Bonheur (*100 days of happiness*) 2007
Vaincre la dépendance affective (*Conquer emotional dependence*) 2012
20 Secrets des millionaires (*20 secrets the millionaires*) 2012
Memoir d'un auteur québécois (*Memoirs of a Quebecois author*) *2015*
 Vivre heureux au 21e siècle *(How to live happily in the 21st century)* 2009
Available on Amazon

Marc Theriault has been an advisor in financial security for 25 years and has a diploma in finance.

He works as conference lecturer and coach in the field of self-development.

Bibliography
Croire en soi (*Believing in oneself*) by Marc Thériault, Thériault Editions 2005, 292 pages
Dans la jungle du placement (*In the investment jungle*) by Stephen A. Jarislowsky, Transcontinental Editions, 2005, 161 pages.

www.ingramcontent.com/pod-product-compliance
Lightning Source LLC
Chambersburg PA
CBHW071823200526
45169CB00018B/928